Contents

Our world, our place 2

Kangaroo Island 4

Too many tourists 7

The northern hairy-nosed wombat 10

My Sitting Down Place 14

Strands in action 16

Our world, our place

Nature surrounds us, from parks and backyards, to streets and alleyways. Next time you go out for a walk, tread gently and remember that we are both inhabitants and ***stewards*** *of nature in our neighbourhoods.*

David Suzuki

Our world is home to many plants, animals and humans. Our environment provides us with shelter, food, water and enjoyment. Some people like to take walks to enjoy the **flora** and **fauna** in nature. Other people have special places that are important because of their beliefs and culture. Many people are involved in protecting our world so that plants, animals and humans can continue to live a happy and healthy life.

The natural environment contains many wonders, but it needs to be looked after.

Did you know?
Through Dreaming stories Aboriginal people understand they have an obligation to look after the land. This has been passed down as law for thousands of years.

stewards people who are responsible for looking after something or someone
flora flowers
fauna animals

A penguin nesting in a penguin box constructed by volunteers

LET'S FIND OUT

- How does the environment support the lives of plants, animals and people?
- Why is it important to look after our environment?
- What are some of the reasons plants and animals become endangered?
- How do people connect with their environment?
- What can we do to protect different environments?

Brochure

Kangaroo Island

Imagine the sound of waves rolling onto the sand, birds circling overhead and the freshness of a sea breeze. Smell the sweetness of Ligurian bee honey and taste the creaminess of soft sheep's cheese. If you love to explore the outdoors and enjoy taste sensations from local producers, then come to Kangaroo Island and be surprised.

Location

Kangaroo Island is located off the coast of South Australia. It is the third-largest Australian coastal island. It was discovered by Captain Matthew Flinders in 1802. Shortly afterwards, people started living on Kangaroo Island. Kangaroo Island now has a population of 4600. Farming and tourism provide the island's two main sources of income.

Travelling to Kangaroo Island

Kangaroo Island can be reached by sea or air. It is a 45-minute ferry trip from Cape Jervis, South Australia, or a 30-minute flight from Adelaide.

Ligurian bee A bee imported from Italy in 1884. The Ligurian bees on Kangaroo Island are the only known colony in the world.

Places to visit

Kangaroo Island has many beautiful places to see. Visit Seal Bay to see the Australian sea lions at play. At Remarkable Rocks you can walk among the magnificent and unusually shaped granite rocks. Perhaps you might like to try sandboarding down the Little Sahara dunes.

The Remarkable Rocks are composed of granite and were formed over 5 million years ago.

Flora and fauna

There is so much wildlife to see! Kangaroo Island has many kangaroos, although they are smaller than their mainland cousins, the Australian grey kangaroo. It also is home to the heath goanna, echidnas, koalas and New Zealand fur seals. There are 46 species of plants found only on Kangaroo Island.

Of course, there are many kangaroos on Kangaroo Island! These are western grey kangaroos.

Protecting nature

Here are some tips for helping to protect local plants and animals:

- stick to walking trails
- clean your boots after walks
- take your rubbish with you
- avoid driving at night as there is a lot of wildlife out at this time.

Breakaway tasks

Remembering

1 List three animals found on Kangaroo Island.
2 Name the two ways that people can travel to the island.

Understanding

3 What is the purpose of a travel brochure?
4 Explain three reasons why people might visit Kangaroo Island.

Applying

5 Write a fact file about one of the places your family likes to visit. Include the name, location, interesting facts and explain why it's a favourite place to visit.

Analysing

6 Find out about Australian sea lions and New Zealand fur seals. Use a Venn diagram to show the similarities and differences.
7 Research some information about the Ligurian bee. Complete the Draw it organiser with words and images to show what is important about this bee.

Evaluating

8 Consider the two ways of reaching Kangaroo Island. Use a PMI (plus, minus and interesting) chart to evaluate the best way of travelling to the island.
9 Talk with a partner about whether or not you would like to visit Kangaroo Island. Explain your choice.

Creating

10 Create a poster for tourists that clearly explains some of the tips that help protect Kangaroo Island's plants and animals.

Too many tourists

Australia is home to some of the most stunning scenery in the world. One area of great beauty is the Great Barrier Reef. It is located off the coast of Queensland. It is the largest coral reef in the world and covers 348 000 square kilometres. Sadly, it is being damaged by the 14 million people who visit it every year. We must do something to protect it!

The Great Barrier Reef has been named a World Heritage Site. This means that it must be protected. It is important to many people, including Aboriginal and Torres Strait Islander Peoples.

Today, the Great Barrier Reef is facing many problems. Satellite photos show that the reef is shrinking and that the coral is slowly dying away. One reason for this is the pollution in the water. Water quality is important for the growth of coral. When the water is polluted the number of crown-of–thorns starfish increases and they feed on the coral.

The Great Barrier Reef is being threatened by pollution and too many tourists.

Water pollution is created by the many tourist boats that visit the reef. The more people that visit, the more **pollutants** enter the water. Then there are other problems with visitors who are careless and damage the coral when swimming. Some people even try to take pieces of coral. This is all having a damaging effect on the reef.

We need to do something before the reef disappears! In 2013, the Australian government wrote a report that included a plan to improve the conditions on the reef, but is that enough?

We can help the reef by making sure that tourist companies reduce the amount of pollution they are making. One way we can do this is by limiting tourist numbers. There could also be times when the reef is tourist-free. We must act now, before the reef is gone forever! Together our actions can make a difference!

Reducing the numbers of tourists that visit the Great Barrier Reef will help save it.

pollutants waste and chemicals that dirty the environment

Breakaway tasks

Remembering

1 Where in Australia is the Great Barrier Reef located?

2 How many tourists visit the reef each year?

Understanding

3 Describe what happens to coral when the water is polluted.

4 Complete a concept map about World Heritage Sites.

Applying

5 Locate the Great Barrier Reef and other World Heritage Sites on a world map.

Analysing

6 Write a haiku poem to describe either the healthy or unhealthy coral from the reef.

7 Find out about the crown-of-thorns starfish. Write an explanation about how it is a problem for the Great Barrier Reef.

Evaluating

8 Is it important to save the Great Barrier Reef? Create a survey to find out other people's opinions. Collect the information and present your results.

9 List ways that tourists can be more eco-friendly when visiting the reef. Rank your ideas from most effective to least effective. Explain your choices.

Creating

10 Design and label a Great Barrier Reef sightseeing boat that does not pollute the water.

The northern hairy-nosed wombat

The northern hairy-nosed wombat is a marsupial. This means it has a pouch for its young. It is called a hairy-nosed wombat because its nose is covered with short brown hairs.

Scientific information

Scientific name: *Lasiorhinus krefftii*

Common name: Northern hairy-nosed wombat

Conservation status: Critically endangered (according to the International Redlist of threatened species)

The northern hairy-nosed wombat

Size: 35 centimetres high and 1 metre long

Weight: Up to 35 kilograms (females slightly heavier than males)

Home

Northern hairy-nosed wombats live in burrows. They have short legs and strong claws for digging their burrows. They usually live on their own, but they sometimes share burrows.

Diet

The northern hairy-nosed wombat is a herbivore. It likes to eat different types of grass. It doesn't usually travel very far from its burrow to find food. It has teeth that continue to grow, even when it is old.

---

marsupial a mammal which has a pouch

Breeding

The northern hairy-nosed wombat has one baby each year. Its young stays in the pouch for about nine months.

Location

Northern hairy-nosed wombats were once found in New South Wales and Queensland. Fossils of northern hairy-nosed wombats have also been found in Victoria. They are now only found in Queensland.

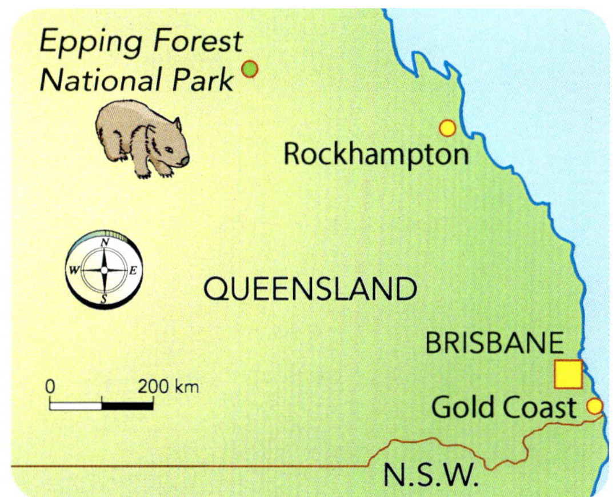

Conservation status

The northern hairy-nosed wombat is now an endangered animal, according to its **conservation status**. There are many reasons why there are very few northern hairy-nosed wombats in the wild. **Drought** has meant that there has not been enough food for them. Some of the wombats' habitats have been destroyed by farming or bushfires.

Conservation status	Description
Extinct	No more animals found in the wild or in captivity
Extinct in the wild	No animals found in the wild
Critically endangered	Extremely high risk of extinction in the wild
Endangered	Very high risk of extinction in the wild
Vulnerable	High risk of extinction in the wild
Near threatened	May be threatened in the near future
Least concern	Many animals are found in the wild
Data deficient	Not enough information is available
Not evaluated	The animal hasn't been evaluated

conservation status indicates whether a species is still alive and how likely it is to become extinct in the near future

drought a time when there is no rain

Increasing numbers

Researchers and park rangers have worked together to try to increase the number of northern hairy-nosed wombats in the wild. In 1971 Epping Forest National Park (Queensland) was formed to protect the wombats' habitat. During 2002 a 20-kilometre fence was built to keep out dingoes.

An unusual solution

The wombats have been helped in one unusual way. Burrows have been constructed for them so they don't need to use all their energy digging a new one. Since Epping Forest National Park was created wombat numbers have increased.

Providing wombats with constructed burrows means they can save their energy for finding food. Permanent traps are set up in Epping Forest National park in order to track wombats and monitor their health.

The future

The wombats' risk of extinction is still high. They will continue to need protection and help if they are to avoid becoming extinct.

Interesting facts

- The northern hairy-nosed wombat is the largest herbivorous burrowing mammal in the world.
- Some burrows can be up to 4 metres deep.
- Northern hairy-nosed wombats can run at up to 40 kilometres per hour over short distances.

Breakaway tasks

Remembering

1 List the states in which northern hairy-nosed wombats used to be found.

2 How have the wombats' habitats been destroyed?

Understanding

3 Explain why Epping Forest National Park was created.

4 Draw a picture of a northern hairy-nosed wombat and label its important features.

Applying

5 What might happen to the northern hairy-nosed wombat if the fence around Epping Forest National Park is removed?

6 Find out about some other Australian animals that are endangered and how they are being helped.

Analysing

7 Write a list of questions about the northern hairy-nosed wombat. Research the answers to your questions.

8 Use a matrix to compare the features of the three types of wombats: northern hairy-nosed wombat, southern hairy-nosed wombat and bare-nosed wombat.

Evaluating

9 Find out how many wombats need to be in the wild for them not to be considered endangered. Estimate how long this might take. You could write to the Epping Forest National Park rangers for information.

Creating

10 Design a safe home for a northern hairy-nosed wombat. Build it using plasticine or modelling clay. Explain the important features.

My Sitting Down Place

by Gail Kay

I go down to the creek
Where the water gurgles
Joyfully
As it hurries along
Over the shining sand and pebbles
To its destiny
With the sea.
Dappled sunlight
Flits and moves
Across the water, over the creek bank,
And the birds sing happily
To the accompaniment
Of insects and crickets.
I sit in silence as I soak it all into my soul.
Peace flows
From the water
To my heart.
Whatever life brings me
I now can face
Because of this,
My sitting down place!

Breakaway tasks

Remembering

1 Make a list of creatures that can be heard in the poem.

2 Find and record five descriptive words from the poem.

Understanding

3 Explain why the poet likes to sit by the creek.

4 Write a concrete poem using words to describe water in a creek.

Applying

5 Draw a picture of the sitting down place that is described in the poem.

6 Write a description of one of your favourite places.

7 Create six interview questions about favourite quiet places. Interview a friend and present your findings in an interesting way.

Analysing

8 Survey other students to find out their favourite places in nature. Make a graph showing your results.

Evaluating

9 Explain why it is important for some people to have a quiet place for thinking.

Creating

10 Create a photo slide show of your favourite places. Choose one word to describe each slide and also include sound effects or music.

Strands in action

Core tasks

1 Find out about places in your community that are important to others.
   a Draw a map to show where the places are located.
   b Interview people about each place.
2 Find out about World Heritage Sites around the world.
   a Create a table that includes the site, the country it is found in, why it is important and any issues.
   b Choose one World Heritage Site and research it. Present it as a report.
   c Share a photo of your chosen World Heritage Site.
   d Present your information to others.

Extra tasks

1 Choose a favourite outdoor place. Use a spider diagram to make a list of words you associate with that place.
2 Write an A–Z of Australian plants and animals.
3 Environments are important to both animals and people. Create a Venn diagram to show why the environment is important to both groups.
4 Find out about a local endangered animal. Write an email or a letter to a supporting foundation to find out what people are doing to help.

The use of alliteration can help to bring descriptive writing to life. Alliteration is the repetition of the same sounds or same letter at the beginning of connected words. For example: The wild, woolly wombat wriggled free to a land of new hope.